SPOT 50
Dogs

Camilla de la Bedoyere

Miles Kelly

First published in 2011 by Miles Kelly Publishing Ltd
Harding's Barn, Bardfield End Green, Thaxted, Essex, CM6 3PX, UK

This edition printed in 2012

2 4 6 8 10 9 7 5 3 1

Publishing Director Belinda Gallagher
Creative Director Jo Cowan
Editor Sarah Parkin
Designer Kayleigh Allen
Production Manager Elizabeth Collins
Reprographics Stephan Davis, Jennifer Hunt

ISBN 978-1-84810-600-0

Printed in China

British Library Cataloguing-in-Publication Data
A catalogue record for this book is available from the British Library

ACKNOWLEDGEMENTS
The publishers would like to thank the artist Ian Jackson who has contributed to this book

All other images are from the Miles Kelly Archives

Made with paper from a sustainable forest

www.mileskelly.net
info@mileskelly.net

www.factsforprojects.com

CONTENTS

Tick the circles when you have spotted the breeds.

TYPES OF DOG

All tame dogs are descended from wolves. For thousands of years, people have bred dogs to develop types (breeds) with particular characteristics. Dogs with certain personalities or body types were bred to produce puppies with characteristics that were suitable for different roles, from farm dogs to family pets and from assistance dogs to show dogs.

TYPE	CHARACTERISTICS
Hounds	These dogs have been developed for hunting. Some of them hunt using sight, such as Greyhounds, while others use their sense of smell, such as Bloodhounds.
Gundogs	Gundogs were developed to follow hunters, find prey and retrieve birds or other animals that had been shot. They suit country life.
Terriers	These small dogs were bred to chase animals that run into burrows, such as badgers, rabbits, rats and foxes. They are usually clever, single-minded, active dogs.
Toy Dogs	Toy dogs tend to be very small. They have been bred to be family pets and companions. These dogs often suit town life and enjoy being with families.
Utility Dogs	These dogs come from mixed backgrounds and may have history of being both companion and working dogs. They are usually friendly and obedient.
Working Dogs	This is a large group of dog breeds. Working dogs are usually obedient and energetic. They are intelligent, so they can be trained, and are affectionate.

Pedigree or mongrel?

A pedigree dog is one that belongs to a particular breed, such as Chihuahua or Dalmatian. A female from one breed may be mated with a male from a different breed. The cross-bred puppies might have characteristics of both parents. A mongrel is a dog that has no obvious pedigree and may be descended from many types of dog.

Male German Spitz

Cross-bred puppy

Female Cavalier King Charles Spaniel

ANATOMY

Dogs are usually described in terms of their body shape and size, and their personalities. The shapes of their heads, muzzles, ears and tails are also used to distinguish breeds.

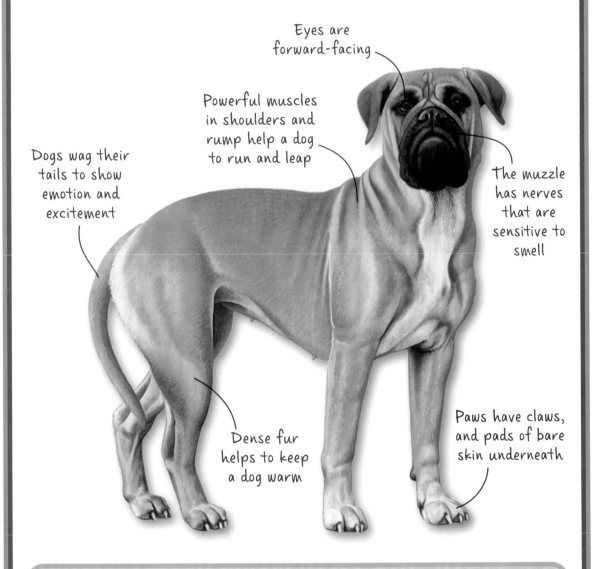

Eyes are forward-facing

Powerful muscles in shoulders and rump help a dog to run and leap

The muzzle has nerves that are sensitive to smell

Dogs wag their tails to show emotion and excitement

Dense fur helps to keep a dog warm

Paws have claws, and pads of bare skin underneath

Measuring dogs

Dogs are measured to their withers, which are the highest points of their shoulders. Most pedigree dogs that are entered into competitions are expected to fall into a 'perfect' size range, which might include weight as well as height. For family dogs, there is no perfect size. The sizes given in this book are a guide to the average size for a particular breed.

180 cm

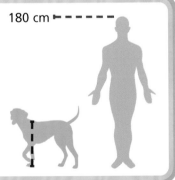

AFGHAN

This ancient breed was once used for hunting. Afghan hounds combine strength, speed and stubbornness. They have a characteristic body shape with long, lean legs and expressive eyes. Afghan fur grows long and silky and needs regular grooming to stay in top condition. These hounds may behave coolly towards strangers, but are very loyal to their owners. Afghans can be difficult to train.

SCALE

This powerful breed originated in the cold mountains of Afghanistan, where a long or thick coat was essential for survival.

FACT FILE

Height 63–74 cm

Colour Black, brown, red, white, tan, blue, grey and mixed colours

Characteristics Shy and loyal

Special feature Long, silky fur

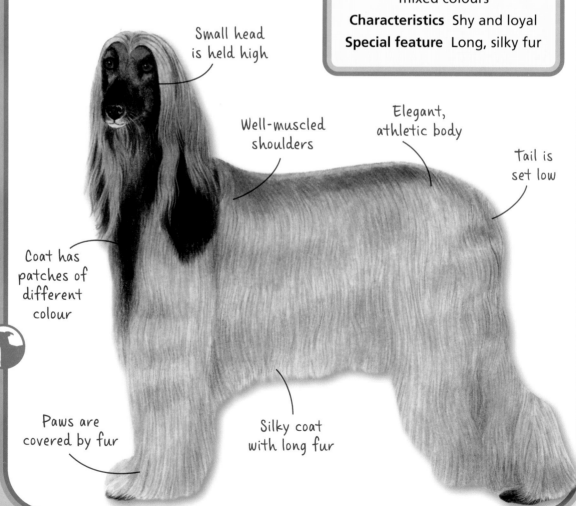

Small head is held high

Well-muscled shoulders

Elegant, athletic body

Tail is set low

Coat has patches of different colour

Paws are covered by fur

Silky coat with long fur

BASSET

These hounds have large, heavy bodies on short legs. Bassets were originally bred to hunt hares and they have an extremely good sense of smell. They have independent minds, which can make them difficult to train. However, Bassets like company and enjoy playing. They can be noisy and may bark loudly if worried, lonely or excited. Bassets sometimes have problems with their hearing and the joints in their legs.

SCALE

According to legend, one of the earliest Basset Hounds was given to the first US president, George Washington, as a gift.

FACT FILE

Height 33–38 cm
Colour Black, tan and white
Characteristics
Playful and friendly
Special feature Stumpy legs

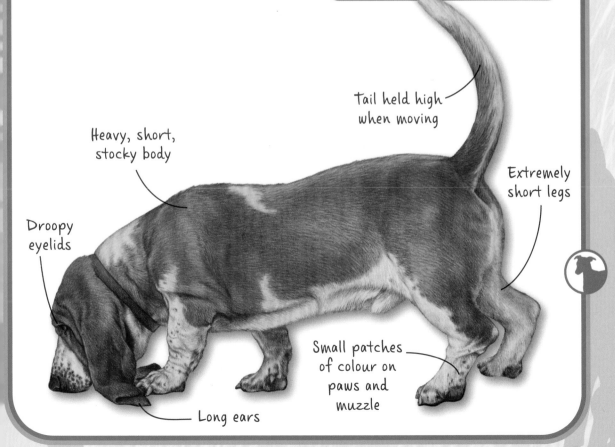

Tail held high when moving

Heavy, short, stocky body

Extremely short legs

Droopy eyelids

Small patches of colour on paws and muzzle

Long ears

BEAGLE

Like other hounds, Beagles are active, energetic dogs with good appetites. They can be difficult to train, especially if they have developed bad habits. Beagles are intelligent, enjoy being around people and are loyal to their owners. They have a good sense of smell and enjoy sniffing everything.

SCALE

In Elizabethan times, tiny Beagles, called Pocket Beagles, were bred to be taken hunting. They were put in saddlebags and carried on horses.

FACT FILE

Height 33–40 cm
Colour Black, tan and white
Characteristics
Sociable and good-natured
Special feature
Energetic hunter

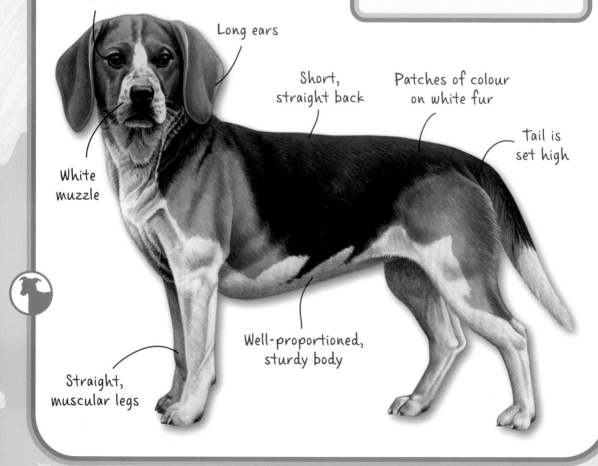

Eyes are hazel or brown

Long ears

Short, straight back

Patches of colour on white fur

Tail is set high

White muzzle

Well-proportioned, sturdy body

Straight, muscular legs

BLOODHOUND

Despite their name and size, **Bloodhounds are sweet-natured, loving dogs.** They have a superb sense of smell, which is why they are used for tracking. Bloodhounds need plenty of food to support their great bodies, but they should only eat small, regular meals to prevent a painful stomach disorder. These large hounds are friendly and enjoy playing. Training takes patience and time.

SCALE

Bloodhounds were once used not just to find the scent of animals, but of people, too – especially escaped prisoners.

FACT FILE

Height 58–69 cm
Colour Tan
Characteristics
Gentle and patient
Special feature
Superb sense of smell

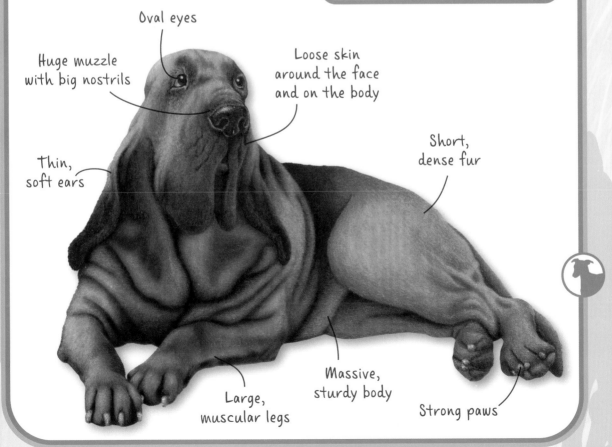

Oval eyes

Huge muzzle with big nostrils

Loose skin around the face and on the body

Short, dense fur

Thin, soft ears

Massive, sturdy body

Large, muscular legs

Strong paws

BORZOI

Also known as Russian Wolfhounds, Borzois are suited to chasing and catching other animals. They have long, powerful jaws and lean, muscular legs. Although Borzois can be friendly and good-natured, they can also show their wilder side. These hounds can be difficult to train for obedience.

SCALE

In the 19th century it was against the law for Russian people to buy a Borzoi. They could only have one if it had been given to them by a Tzar, a Russian ruler.

FACT FILE

Height 68–74 cm

Colour Various including gold, grey, red or patched

Characteristics
Stubborn and calm

Special feature Fast runner

Small, slender head

Patches of red on white fur

Elegant, graceful body

Long jaws

Long, silky fur

Low-set tail

Thick 'feathering' on belly

DACHSHUND

These hounds are small in height, but big in personality. Dachshunds were bred as hunting dogs, as their long, low bodies were ideal for chasing prey into tunnels. Today, they are popular family pets because they are loyal and intelligent. Dachshunds need to learn how to behave around children and other animals from an early age. They can be difficult to train and are sometimes unfriendly to strangers.

SCALE

Dachshunds were first bred in Germany, where they are the national dog. A Dachshund was used as the symbol for Munich's Olympic Games in 1972.

FACT FILE

Weight 9–12 kg (These dogs are not measured in height)

Colour
Brown, or black and tan

Characteristics
Clever and bossy

Special feature Short legs

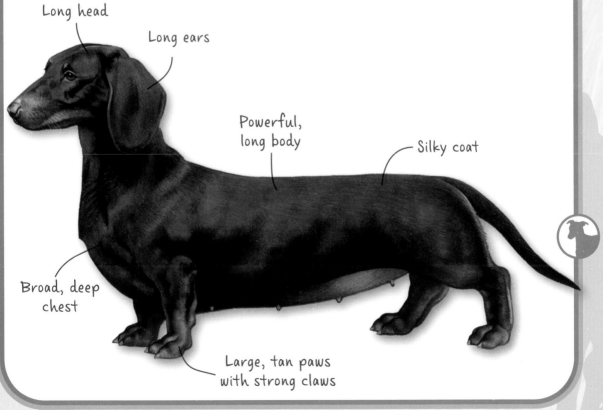

Long head

Long ears

Powerful, long body

Silky coat

Broad, deep chest

Large, tan paws with strong claws

FOXHOUND

English **Foxhounds were bred to take part in fox hunts.** They have great energy and can keep running for several hours without a break. Many Foxhounds are kept as family pets, but they are demanding as they require a lot of exercise and they love to be outdoors. Foxhounds are pack animals, so they like to live and exercise in a group.

SCALE

According to legend, it was a faithful Foxhound called Old Drum that led to the famous phrase 'a dog is a man's best friend'.

FACT FILE

Height 58–64 cm
Colour Tan, black and white
Characteristics
Energetic and sociable
Special feature A pack animal

Broad, alert face

Long muzzle

Hardy, strong body

Coat can be in two or three colours

The tail is set high

Straight legs with round paws

White fur on legs

GREYHOUND

Unlike some hounds, Greyhounds use sight to follow prey rather than a keen sense of smell. These dogs love to chase moving things, which is why they are used in dog racing. Greyhounds are bred to run fast, although as family pets they also need to have calm, loveable natures. Greyhounds are not suitable for families that have other small animals, such as cats or rabbits.

SCALE

Racing greyhounds can reach speeds of about 65 km/h – that is faster than most horses run.

FACT FILE

Height 68–76 cm

Colour Black, white, red, blue, brown, reddish-yellow

Characteristics
Affectionate and athletic

Special feature Fast runner

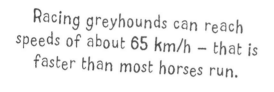

Alert eyes

Small ears

Long muzzle

Slender, elegant, athletic body

Pale brown fur is called fawn

Long tail with a fine point

Thin but strong legs

Small paws

IRISH WOLFHOUND

This is one of the largest breeds of dog and also one of the gentlest. Irish Wolfhounds were first bred to hunt wolves and other large animals. However, those early dogs probably did not reach the great sizes seen today. These hounds are affectionate, but can be difficult to look after because of their size.

SCALE

Roman warriors, including Julius Caesar, are said to have used Irish Wolfhounds in battle to attack enemy chariots.

FACT FILE

Height 71–79 cm

Colour Grey, red, black, white or fawn

Characteristics Gentle and calm

Special feature Huge size

Large head

Small, dark eyes

Small ears

Long neck

Powerful, muscular body

Long muzzle

Deep chest

Long tail

Muscular legs with large paws

Shaggy fur

WHIPPET

These dogs are one of the friendliest and most loyal of all hounds. Whippets have patient natures and quickly learn to adore their owners. They are fast runners and love to hunt. Curious, alert and active, whippets are always on the lookout for something to chase. Whippets are sometimes known as 'Snapdogs' because they can kill a rat with a single snap of their jaws.

SCALE

Like greyhounds, whippets are often raced around courses for sport. They were once known as 'poor men's racehorses'.

FACT FILE

Height 44–51 cm

Colour Black, brown, red, white, tan, blue, grey and mixed colours

Characteristics Intelligent and patient

Special feature Small but fast

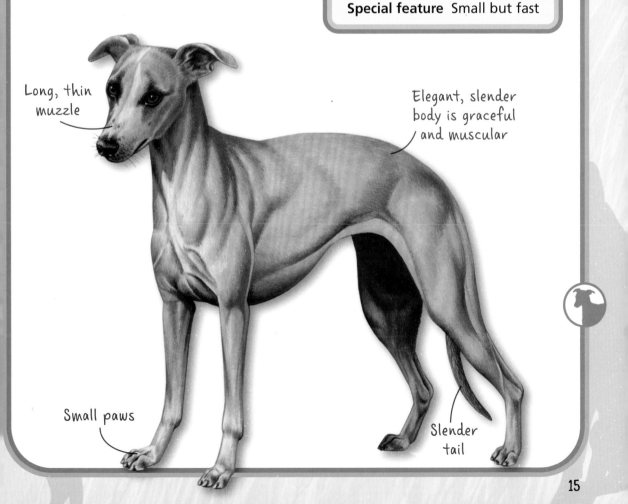

Long, thin muzzle

Elegant, slender body is graceful and muscular

Small paws

Slender tail

ENGLISH COCKER SPANIEL

These curious, active dogs love to sniff and explore. English Cocker Spaniels were originally bred to accompany hunters and find birds or other animals that had been shot. They are friendly family pets that love to be kept busy, especially by catching, fetching and playing. Cocker Spaniels have silky fur, which grows long around their legs, so they need to be groomed regularly.

SCALE

Cocker Spaniels do not make good guard dogs. They are more likely to lick a stranger than bark or growl!

FACT FILE

Height 38–41 cm
Colour Orange or black
Characteristics
Charming and companionable
Special feature
Loves to carry things

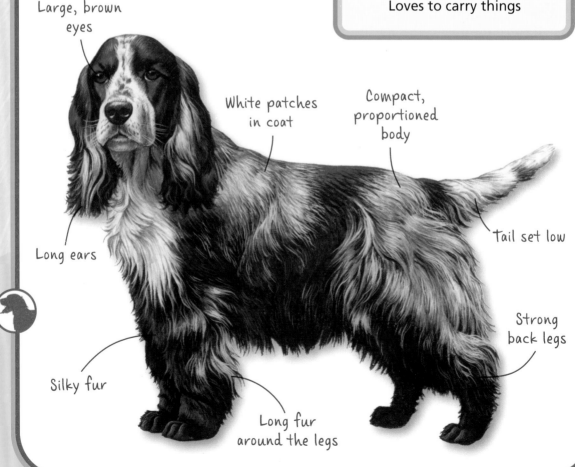

Large, brown eyes

White patches in coat

Compact, proportioned body

Tail set low

Long ears

Strong back legs

Silky fur

Long fur around the legs

GOLDEN RETRIEVER

Popular and loveable, these dogs were first bred from Spaniels, Labrador Retrievers and Red Setters. Golden Retrievers have developed into a breed of reliable, intelligent and trusting dogs. They are often used as working dogs, especially assistance dogs, because they are obedient and quick to learn. Golden Retrievers are known for their gentle natures, so they are especially popular as family pets. They love to play, fetch and chew, and also enjoy swimming.

SCALE

Golden Retrievers have been bred with Poodles to produce a new variety of intelligent dog that does not shed too much hair – Goldendoodles.

FACT FILE

Height 52–61 cm
Colour Cream or golden
Characteristics
Obedient and intelligent
Special feature
Works as an assistance dog

Eyes are set well apart

Long, strong body

Top coat has wavy fur

Large muzzle

Round paws

IRISH SETTER

First bred as hunting dogs, Irish Setters have **an excellent sense of smell.** They are known for their great beauty and elegance. Their chestnut coat can be groomed until it shines and is silky to the touch. Irish Setters are energetic and easily distracted. They love to chase and sniff, but it can be difficult to get them to return when called, so training is important.

SCALE

Irish Setters were once bred in a range of colours including red, red and white, lemon, or white with brown patches.

FACT FILE

Height 61–65 cm

Colour Chestnut

Characteristics
Enthusiastic and affectionate

Special feature
A beautiful coat

Almond-shaped eyes

Elegant, slender head

Muscular, graceful body

Long jaws

Long, silky fur

Strong legs

LABRADOR RETRIEVER

The first Labrador Retrievers worked with hunters and fishermen. They have become popular family pets because they have friendly personalities and great intelligence. These dogs can be trained and are obedient. They work with the police, as trackers, or as assistance dogs. Labrador Retrievers enjoy any chance to swim or fetch balls from a pond. Their coats are waterproof, so they do not mind getting wet.

SCALE

Labradors originally came from Canada and they are still popular there. Most of the assistance dogs in Canada are Labrador Retrievers.

FACT FILE

Height 54–57 cm

Colour Black, chocolate or yellow

Characteristics Sociable and affectionate

Special feature Loves water

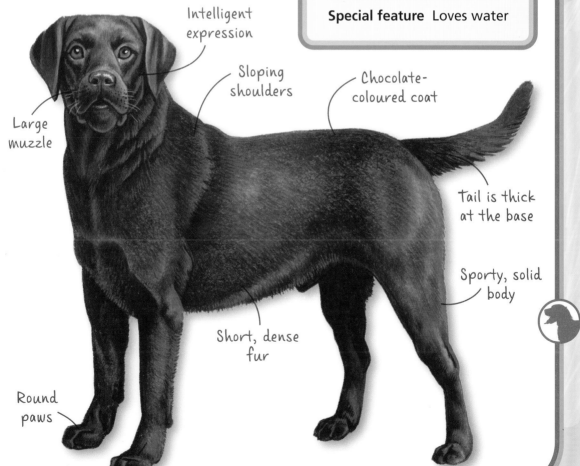

Intelligent expression

Sloping shoulders

Chocolate-coloured coat

Large muzzle

Tail is thick at the base

Sporty, solid body

Short, dense fur

Round paws

POINTER

These dogs enjoy company and being kept busy. Pointers were bred to accompany hunters, often to chase animals such as rabbits and hares. They stand and stare, or 'point', at their prey. Pointers have athletic bodies and love to run and chase. These dogs need plenty of time outdoors, but they are also happy in the home and like children. Pointers need company and they may become destructive if left alone for long.

SCALE

Pointers often worked with other dogs. They would find the prey, but Greyhounds or Retrievers would be sent to chase or collect it.

FACT FILE

Height 61–69 cm
Colour White with lemon, orange, brown or black patches
Characteristics
Friendly and active
Special feature 'Points' at prey

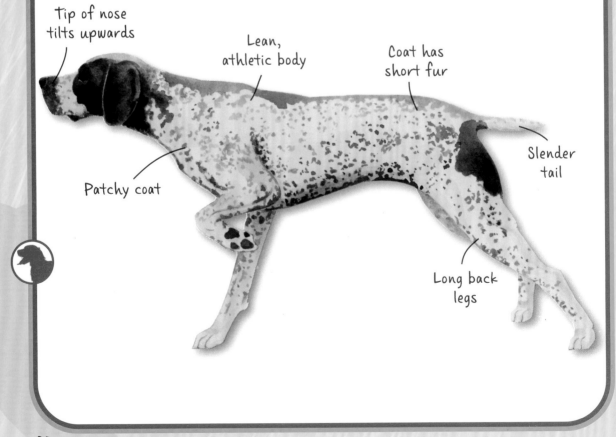

Tip of nose tilts upwards

Lean, athletic body

Coat has short fur

Patchy coat

Slender tail

Long back legs

WEIMARANER

This breed was developed in Germany. Weimaraners were once popular as hunting dogs. Today they are kept as pets and show dogs, because they have a good nature and an unusual appearance. They are sometimes called 'grey ghosts', because of the strange but beautiful grey-brown colour of their coats. Weimaraners are friendly dogs, but they bark at strangers, which makes them good guard dogs.

SCALE

These family dogs may become anxious or scared if left alone for periods of time.

FACT FILE

Height 56–69 cm

Colour Grey

Characteristics
Energetic and sharp

Special feature Eyes are blue or amber in colour

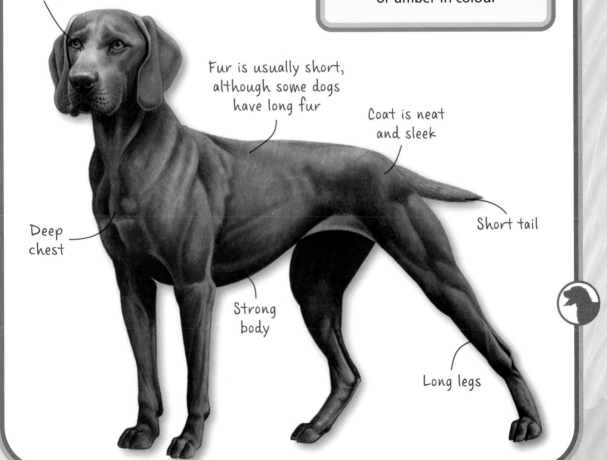

Blue eyes

Fur is usually short, although some dogs have long fur

Coat is neat and sleek

Deep chest

Short tail

Strong body

Long legs

BORDER TERRIER

Terriers were first bred to accompany hunters and chase or catch animals. Border Terriers were fast runners, but they were also small enough to chase foxes down their holes. Today, Border Terriers are kept as family pets. They love to play and are good companions for children. Border Terriers are obedient, but need firm training as they have lively spirits.

SCALE

These little dogs are named after the Borders region, which marks the boundary between England and Scotland, where the breed developed.

FACT FILE

Height 28–30 cm

Colour Red, brown, fawn and tan

Characteristics Good-natured

Special feature Strong hunting instinct

Rounded head

Usually has dark ears, muzzle and eyes

Moustache

Long, wiry fur feels rough

Sturdy, active body

Strong claws

PARSON JACK RUSSELL

Jack Russell Terriers are descended from Fox **Terriers.** They were bred by a parson called Reverend John Russell. He wanted a dog that could chase a fox into a hole, but that had long enough legs to run beside a horse. The breed has been popular ever since. These dogs are intelligent, but need firm training. They also need to spend time with people when they are young to become patient, calm and obedient.

SCALE

These Terriers are unusually long-lived and have been known to reach the age of 20 years or more.

FACT FILE

Height 28–38 cm
Colour White with lemon, tan or black markings
Characteristics
Stubborn and affectionate
Special feature Loves to dig

Bright and alert expression

Ears droop forwards

Tan patches

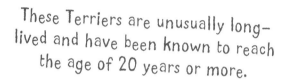

Long tail is set high

Strong body

Long, strong legs

SCOTTISH TERRIER

These Terriers are also known as Scottie
Dogs. They are usually black, although
other colours do exist. Scottish Terriers are
surprisingly bold for their size and, like other
Terriers, they can be stubborn. They have a
sweet appearance, but sometimes have short
tempers and do not like being teased. Scottish
Terriers are intelligent and loyal to their
owners, but can be difficult to train.

SCALE

Scotties are also known as Aberdeen
Terriers. They are one of several
breeds of Terrier that were
developed in Scotland.

FACT FILE

Height 25–28 cm

Colour Black

Characteristics
Friendly and fearless

Special feature
Skilled at catching rats

Long-haired
eyebrows

Tall ears

Thick tail is
held upright

Long neck

Solid,
thick-set
body

Wiry coat

Long fur on
the muzzle
and legs

Short legs

STAFFORDSHIRE BULL TERRIER

Staffies, as they are often known, belong to an English breed that was developed by mixing Bulldogs and Terriers. They have been bred to become incredibly powerful dogs. Staffies were once used for dog-fighting and catching rats, but now they are popular pets. Although these dogs are affectionate and loving, they can be stubborn and do not get on well with other dogs. They need firm training and lots of exercise.

SCALE

These Terriers became popular when putting dogs to fight with bears and bulls became illegal, but dog-fighting was still allowed.

FACT FILE

Height 35–41 cm

Colour Fawn, red, brown or black

Characteristics Boisterous and bold

Special feature Strength

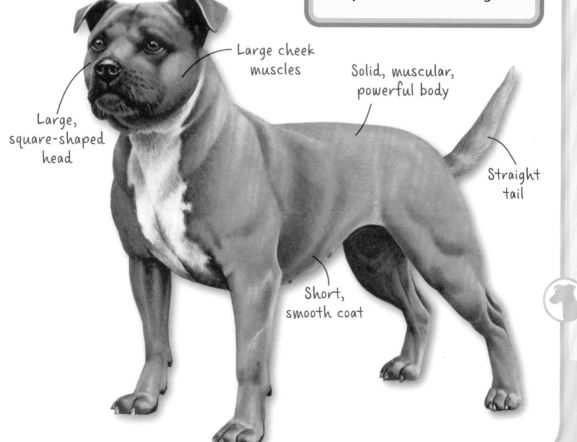

Large cheek muscles

Solid, muscular, powerful body

Large, square-shaped head

Straight tail

Short, smooth coat

WIRE FOX TERRIER

Most Terriers tend to be stubborn and the Wire Fox Terrier is no exception. Terriers were bred to fix their attention on their prey, so they are not easily distracted. Wire Fox Terriers have lots of energy and personality. If they are used to being with children from a young age, they become very sociable and patient. They like to play and love to dig.

SCALE

Tintin is a character in a series of comic books that have sold all over the world. He has a Wire Fox Terrier called Snowy.

FACT FILE

Height 39 cm maximum

Colour White or tan with black markings

Characteristics
Brave and sociable

Special feature
Healthy and long-lived

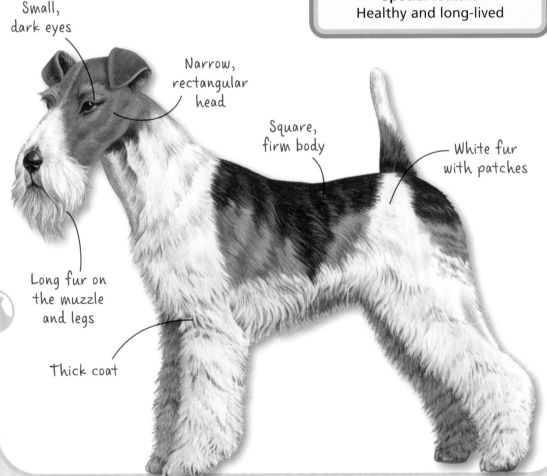

Small, dark eyes

Narrow, rectangular head

Square, firm body

White fur with patches

Long fur on the muzzle and legs

Thick coat

BICHON FRISE

Little Bichon Frise dogs are always white and have thick, fluffy coats. They are kept as companion dogs, but are also popular as show dogs. These dogs require grooming to keep their fur in top condition. Their coat can either be allowed to grow long and curly, or trimmed short. Good-natured, these dogs make perfect pets for caring children and they do not need much exercise.

SCALE

It is believed that Bichon Frise dogs were bred in Tenerife, in the Canary Islands, and they were popular with members of European royal families.

FACT FILE

Height 23–28 cm

Colour White

Characteristics
Happy and lively

Special feature
Thick white coat

Long, arched neck

Raised, curved tail

Rounded head with a strong jaw

Small, rounded paws

Small, solid, square-shaped body

CAVALIER KING CHARLES SPANIEL

These charming little dogs are named after an English King, Charles II, who loved the breed. They are popular dogs and are simple to care for. Cavalier King Charles Spaniels are easy to train and eager to please. They make good family pets and are welcoming to strangers. These dogs are similar to King Charles Spaniels.

SCALE

Cavaliers are slightly bigger than King Charles Spaniels and have less domed heads. They also have longer noses.

FACT FILE

Height Around 32 cm

Colour White and tan, black and tan, black

Characteristics
Easy-going and affectionate

Special feature
Long, feathery ears

Large eyes with gentle expression

Straight back

Patches of tan fur

Furry tail

Long ears

Elegant, athletic body

Silky long fur, especially around the legs

CHIHUAHUA

It is thought that modern Chihuahuas are **descended from an older South or Central American breed of tiny dog.** They are one of the smallest breeds, but they have big personalities and are brave and friendly. Chihuahuas have small appetites and need several small meals throughout the day. If they are looked after well, Chihuahuas can live longer than most dogs and may reach 20 years of age.

SCALE

Chihuahua puppies have tiny stomachs and need to be fed at least every three hours. If they are left too long without food, they quickly become ill or die.

FACT FILE

Height 15–23 cm

Colour Black, brown, red, tan, fawn, grey and white

Characteristics Spirited

Special feature Very long-lived

Small, domed head

Large ears

Attractive face with large eyes

Tail held high when moving

Small, sturdy body

Long-haired coat

Dainty paws

CHINESE CRESTED DOG

There are two types of Chinese Crested Dogs. One type has long, soft hair all over its body and is called a Powder Puff. The other type is hairless, except for the hair on its head, neck, tail and feet. Both types of dog have a contented nature and are easy to look after. They are happy to exercise by playing in the garden and enjoy being with children.

SCALE

Despite their name, these unique dogs probably did not originate in China. It is thought they were first bred in Africa, before becoming popular elsewhere.

FACT FILE

Height 23–33 cm
Colour Usually white or silvery white
Characteristics Cheerful and sociable
Special feature Hairless

Large ears

Hairless skin

Fine hair on the head and neck

Tail has hair

Patches of colour on the skin

Hairy feet

GRIFFON BRUXELLOIS

This little dog is also known as the Brussels Griffon. Griffons were originally bred for catching rats, especially around stables. They are probably descended from a mixture of breeds, including Pugs, Spaniels and Terriers. Although they are fun-loving companion dogs, they are not ideal pets for children as they are sensitive and easily frightened. Griffons are clever, easy to train and loyal to their owners.

SCALE

A Griffon Bruxellois can be bred with a Bichon Frise to produce puppies called Griffichons. They are well-behaved family pets.

FACT FILE

Height 18–20 cm
Colour Red or black
Characteristics
Shy and stubborn
Special feature
Walrus-like moustache

Round head

Small, pug-like face

Stumpy, solid body

Fur is wiry

Walrus-like moustache

Neat, little legs

PAPILLON

Little Papillon dogs are named after the French word for butterfly, because their large ears look like butterfly wings. They are usually kept as companion dogs or to show at competitions, but some Papillons also work as assistance dogs. This is an old breed and Papillons were once popular with royal families of Europe. Today, they make good family pets as they are friendly, clever, obedient and loving.

SCALE

Papillons may be small, but they are strong and athletic. They may compete in dog agility trials, where dogs race and jump around courses.

FACT FILE

Height 20–28 cm

Colour White with patches of colour

Characteristics Alert and active

Special feature Large ears

Large, feathery ears look like butterfly wings

A blaze of white on the forehead looks like a butterfly's body

Small, delicate face

Dainty, delicate body

Furry tail

Long, silky fur

PEKINGESE

These dogs are named after the Chinese city of Beijing, which was once known as Peking. Pekes, as they are often called, were kept by the Chinese royal family and ordinary people were forbidden to own one. Eventually, some Pekes were taken out of China and one was presented to British Queen Victoria. Pekes are well-mannered and like being with families. They do not particularly enjoy exercising and prefer walking to running.

SCALE

These dogs are sometimes called 'lion dogs' because they look similar to the lions that appear in Chinese art and legends.

FACT FILE

Height 18 cm

Colour Black, brown, red, tan, fawn, grey and white

Characteristics
Aloof and faithful

Special feature Thick coat of long fur

Large, wide, rounded head

Flat face

Compact, furry body

Long fluffy tail curls over the back

Short, thick neck

Large paws

POMERANIAN

Little Pomeranians need a great deal of grooming. Thankfully, these companion dogs enjoy plenty of attention. They are probably descended from larger working dogs (known as Spitz dogs) that pulled sleds in the Arctic region, and have kept the intelligence of those breeds. Pomeranians are fairly easy to train, but they have to learn to control their desire to yap. They are energetic but do not need a lot of exercise.

SCALE

The first Pomeranians became very popular in the Pomerania region of central Europe, which is now part of Germany and Poland.

FACT FILE

Height 22–28 cm
Colour Orange, black or white
Characteristics
Bouncy and yappy
Special feature Fox-like face

Fox-like face

Long, fluffy tail is held over the body

Fur has a thick undercoat

Short neck

Fragile, compact, miniature body

Fine-boned legs with small paws

PUG

These dogs are small versions of English Mastiffs, which belong to a group of large working dogs. Pugs are bold, proud dogs that have surprisingly heavy bodies. They are popular because they have interesting personalities and their flat faces, with large eyes, are full of expression. Pugs sometimes struggle to cope with hot weather and they can have difficulty breathing because of their short noses.

SCALE

Pugs have large heads, heavy chests and short legs, which means they may not be able to swim. Their body shape can also stop them from chasing balls.

FACT FILE

Height 25–28 cm

Colour Usually fawn

Characteristics
Happy and sociable

Special feature Curled tail

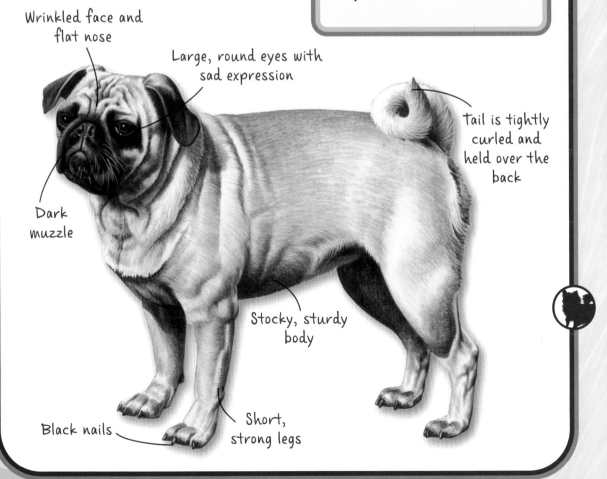

Wrinkled face and flat nose

Large, round eyes with sad expression

Tail is tightly curled and held over the back

Dark muzzle

Stocky, sturdy body

Black nails

Short, strong legs

YORKSHIRE TERRIER

Often known as Yorkies, these dogs are popular as companions and to show in competitions. They have incredible coats of long, silky fur. Yorkshire Terriers are probably descended from a mixture of Terrier breeds, and developed into very small dogs with long fur. They are clever and brave. Despite their size, Yorkshire Terriers will attack dogs much larger than themselves. They are not always patient with children.

SCALE

Very small Yorkshire Terriers, called 'teacups', are sometimes bred, although they have health problems.

A band or ribbon can be used to keep fur out of the dog's eyes

Tall, alert ears

FACT FILE

Height 18–20 cm

Colour Steel blue and bright tan

Characteristics Aloof and intelligent

Special feature Long, silky fur

Straight back

Steel blue fur

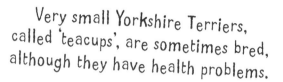

Short muzzle

Tan fur is dark at the roots, but light at the tips

Fur on body is long and glossy

BULLDOG

Also known as the English Bulldog, this is an old breed that was once used in bull and bear fighting. As a result, Bulldogs have large heads, powerful jaws and strong front legs. Modern dogs have been bred to keep the unusual appearance, but to also have affectionate and gentle natures. Bulldogs are good family pets that get on with other animals. They do not like the heat or too much exercise.

SCALE

These proud and powerful dogs are also known as British Bulldogs and are regarded as the national breed.

FACT FILE

Height 23–36 cm

Colour Brown, red, fawn or white

Characteristics Stubborn and affectionate

Special feature Strong head and shoulders

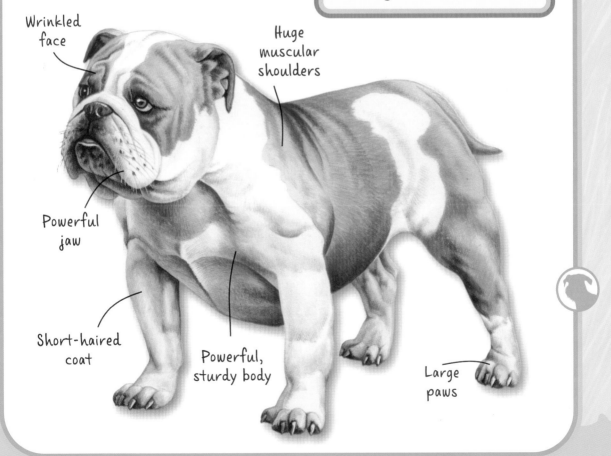

Wrinkled face

Huge muscular shoulders

Powerful jaw

Short-haired coat

Powerful, sturdy body

Large paws

CHOW CHOW

This is an old breed that was probably developed in Mongolia and China. Chow chows were kept as guard and hunting dogs, but today are kept as family pets. These dogs have a reputation for being bad-tempered. However, they can behave very well if they are treated with respect and spend time with strangers and children from an early age. Chow Chows need to be groomed every day.

SCALE

It has been discovered that this is a very ancient breed of dog, and possibly a direct descendent of the first domestic dogs that were bred from wolves.

FACT FILE

Height 46–56 cm

Colour Red, black, blue, fawn, white or cream

Characteristics Aloof and stubborn

Special feature Blue-black tongue

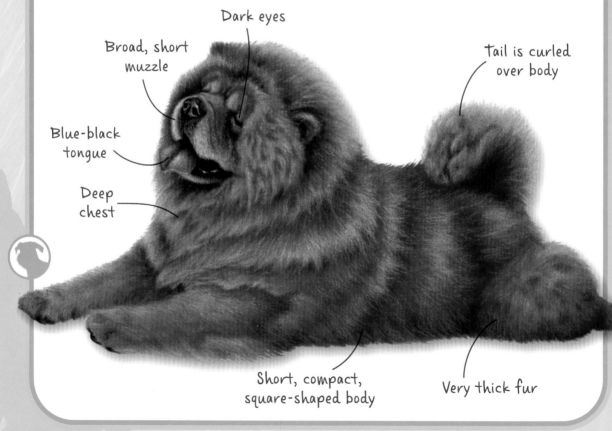

Dark eyes

Broad, short muzzle

Tail is curled over body

Blue-black tongue

Deep chest

Short, compact, square-shaped body

Very thick fur

DALMATIAN

This is one of the oldest breeds of dogs. Their spotted coats make Dalmatians instantly recognizable and much-loved. They used to run alongside carriages and were admired for their athletic beauty, as well as their ability to guard their owners. Dalmatians have delightful personalities and are full of fun-loving energy. They are loyal and love to be praised by their owners.

SCALE

Most Dalmatian puppies are white when they are born. The characteristic spotted coat develops over a number of weeks.

FACT FILE

Height 56–61 cm

Colour White with black or brown spots

Characteristics Outgoing and loyal

Special feature Spotted coat

Eyes are amber or dark

Ears are set high on the head

Level back

Long tail has an upward curve

Intelligent, lively expression

Strong, square body

Short, neat coat

Round paws

LHASA APSO

These dogs were bred in Tibet to work as watchdogs. They needed long, thick coats to protect them from the cold winters. Today, Lhasa Apsos are most admired for their beautiful coats, which need to be groomed every day to avoid matting. They are intelligent and loyal to their owners, but sometimes dislike strangers. Lhasa Apsos enjoy being with children, but they are upset by loud noises.

SCALE

This is an ancient breed that is named after the old Tibetan city of Lhasa. In Tibet, these dogs are known as 'Bearded Lion Dogs'.

FACT FILE

Height 23–28 cm
Colour Usually gold to grey
Characteristics
Trustful and intelligent
Special feature
Healthy and long-lived

Slender head with hair falling over the eyes

Large, fluffy ears

Long back

Long-haired tail is set high and falls over the back

Long beard

Short legs

POODLE

The Standard Poodle is known for its intelligence and obedience. In the past, Poodles were sometimes used as hunting dogs, but they have been kept as family pets for a long time. Their fur does not shed and it is often clipped, because it can grow very long and dense. Standard Poodles have been bred to develop two more types – Miniature and Toy Poodles. All Poodles are good companion dogs, with patient and friendly natures.

SCALE

Toy Poodles are companion dogs that are less than 28 cm tall. They usually live longer than standard poodles and are easy to train.

FACT FILE

Height 38 cm minimum

Colour Black, brown, red, white, tan, blue, grey and mixed colours

Characteristics Lively and happy

Special feature Curly fur

Proud, well-shaped head and face

Long ears

Elegant, slender body

Small, oval paws

Short back

Fur is normally clipped

SCHNAUZER

These dogs were once used to catch rats and to work as guard dogs. They are still known to be wary of strangers, and will defend their homes and owners. Schnauzers can be stubborn, so they need to be well-trained to learn obedience. They are energetic and enjoy lots of exercise. Schnauzers can have up to 15 puppies in a litter and may live to the age of 17 years.

SCALE

Giant and Miniature Schnauzers are also bred. The Giants reach 70 cm in height, while the Miniatures may only be 33 cm tall.

FACT FILE

Height 43–50 cm

Colour Salt and pepper, black or white

Characteristics Active and territorial

Special feature Long eyebrows

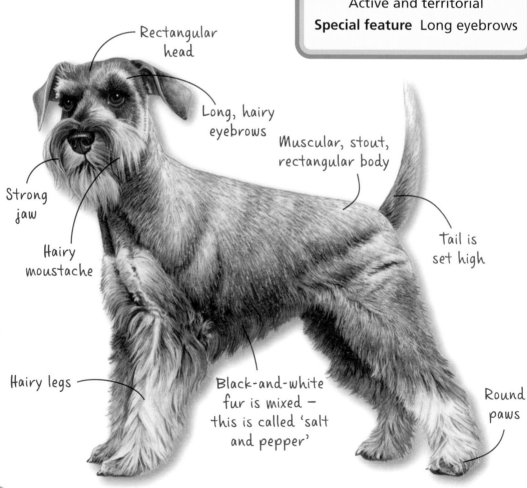

Rectangular head

Long, hairy eyebrows

Muscular, stout, rectangular body

Strong jaw

Hairy moustache

Tail is set high

Hairy legs

Black-and-white fur is mixed — this is called 'salt and pepper'

Round paws

SHAR PEI

First bred in China, this breed nearly died out. Shar Peis have become more popular recently, although they can be difficult to care for. Puppies have wrinkled skin, and although some wrinkles disappear as they grow, the adult dogs still have deep folds of skin around their faces and necks. They often have skin and eye problems. Shar Peis are stubborn dogs. They can be difficult to train and may be bad-tempered.

SCALE

These dogs were once eaten in China and in the 1970s they were regarded as one of the rarest breeds in the world.

FACT FILE

Height 46–51 cm

Colour Black, red, fawn or cream

Characteristics Playful and stubborn

Special feature Wrinkled skin

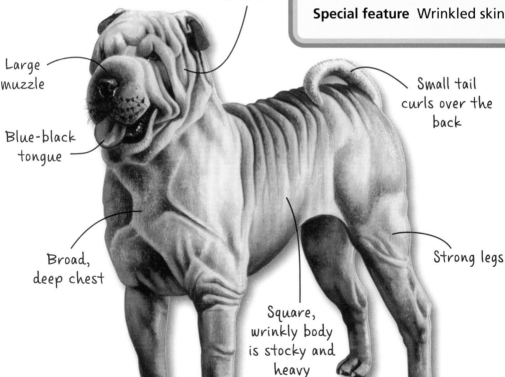

Wrinkled face, neck and shoulders

Large muzzle

Blue-black tongue

Small tail curls over the back

Broad, deep chest

Strong legs

Square, wrinkly body is stocky and heavy

SHIH TZU

First bred in Tibet, Shih Tzu dogs have probably been mixed with Pekingese in the past. They are kept as companion dogs and also to show in competitions. Their long, thick fur needs a lot of grooming to keep it in good condition. Shih Tzus are clever dogs that like to play. However, training them is difficult because they are stubborn and do not always like doing what they are told.

SCALE

The fur on the top of a Shih Tzu's head would cover its eyes if it were not tied up in an arrangement called a 'top knot'.

FACT FILE

Height 23–27 cm

Colour Black, red, grey, gold, brown, silver

Characteristics Independent and clever

Special feature Long fringe

Fur is tied back above eyes

Long, sturdy, small-framed body

Tail is carried over the back

Long fur often has white markings

Short, strong legs

44

BORDER COLLIE

These dogs are often found on farms, helping farmers to herd their sheep or cattle. Border Collies are incredibly intelligent and can be trained to follow commands. They are obedient by nature, so they have also been trained to work with rescue parties and as sniffer dogs. Border Collies are energetic and fast, so they need plenty of exercise.

SCALE

Betsy, a Border Collie from Austria, has become famous because she understands more than 340 words and recognizes 15 people by name.

FACT FILE

Height 51–56 cm
Colour Black and white
Characteristics
Intelligent and active
Special feature
Obedient farm dog

Agile, athletic body

White markings

Coat is smooth and long

Alert, intelligent expression

Legs are short for the body length

Oval-shaped paws

BOXER

Large, fearless Boxers were bred to be hunting and guard dogs. They are now kept as family pets, but will still guard their owners and their homes with courage. Boxers are energetic dogs and need daily exercise. They also have big appetites and need plenty of good food. Despite their size, Boxers are playful dogs and enjoy being kept busy.

SCALE

Boxers were bred from British Bulldogs and German Bullenbeissers – a breed of dog that was used in bull and bear fighting, but no longer exists.

FACT FILE

Height 57–63 cm
Colour Red, fawn, brown or white
Characteristics Lively and bold
Special feature Wrinkled face

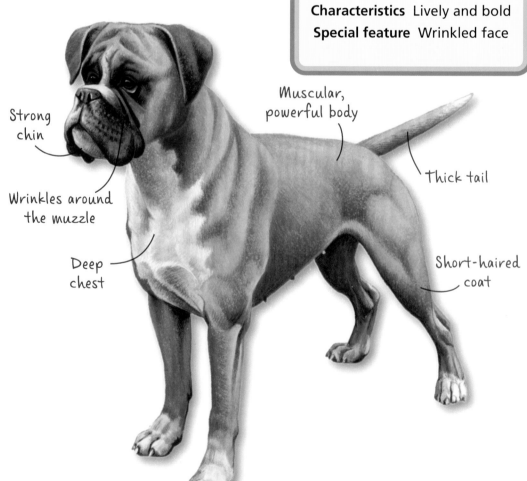

Strong chin

Wrinkles around the muzzle

Deep chest

Muscular, powerful body

Thick tail

Short-haired coat

BULLMASTIFF

Known for their loyalty and strength, Bullmastiffs make excellent guard dogs. They defend their owners and their homes, but are obedient and faithful. Bullmastiffs normally have about eight puppies in a litter and even the puppies are large. They should not have too much exercise because it can damage their growing bones. Young dogs can be stubborn, so they need to be carefully trained.

SCALE

These dogs were bred from Mastiffs and Bulldogs to produce strong but obedient dogs. They were used to overpower poachers and trespassers.

FACT FILE

Height 61–69 cm

Colour Brown, fawn or red

Characteristics
Loyal and reliable

Special feature
Very good guard dog

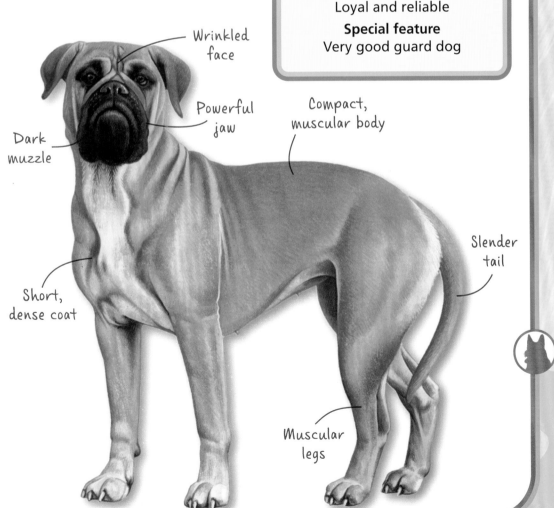

Wrinkled face

Powerful jaw

Compact, muscular body

Dark muzzle

Slender tail

Short, dense coat

Muscular legs

DOBERMANN

These dogs were bred to be guard dogs. It is thought that many different breeds contributed to the Dobermann, including German Shepherds, Terriers, Great Danes and Greyhounds. As a result, Dobermanns combine strength, power and loyalty, as well as beauty and elegance. They are faithful and clever, but are also extremely energetic and require plenty of exercise, food and careful handling.

SCALE

Dobermanns are also known as Dobies and Dobermann Pinschers. They have large litters, with an average of eight puppies at a time.

FACT FILE

Height 63–72 cm

Colour Black with tan markings

Characteristics Intelligent and affectionate

Special feature Often has large litters

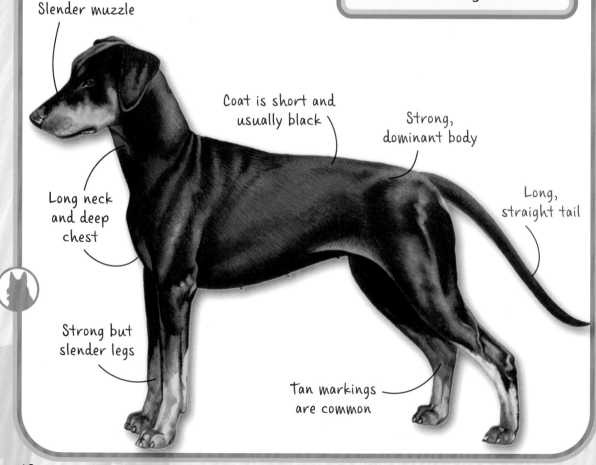

Slender muzzle

Coat is short and usually black

Strong, dominant body

Long, straight tail

Long neck and deep chest

Strong but slender legs

Tan markings are common

GERMAN SHEPHERD DOG

SCALE

Also known as Alsatians, German Shepherds are one of the most popular and recognizable breeds of dog. They are loved as family pets, but they also work for the police as guard or rescue dogs, and often train as assistance dogs. German Shepherds are intelligent and obedient. They are fast learners and form close bonds with their owners.

Today's German Shepherd is a fairly modern breed, even though its appearance is very similar to that of its wolf ancestors.

FACT FILE

Height 55–65 cm

Colour Black, or black with tan markings

Characteristics Obedient

Special feature Intelligent working dog

Intelligent expression

Large, alert ears

Black fur on back

Coat can be medium length or long

Strong, agile, long body

Thick fur on tail

Round paws

GREAT DANE

Developed for hunting large animals, Great Danes required huge, muscular bodies. Today they are used as guard dogs and are family pets. However, their enormous size means they need homes where there is plenty of space and opportunity to exercise. Great Danes are loyal and friendly, and enjoy being around children. Like other big dogs, Great Danes should not have too much exercise while they are growing.

SCALE

In 2010, a Great Dane called Giant George became the world's tallest dog, measuring 109 cm from paw to shoulder.

FACT FILE

Height 71 cm minimum

Colour Brown, fawn, blue, black, or white with dark patches

Characteristics
Lively and friendly

Special feature
A good guard dog

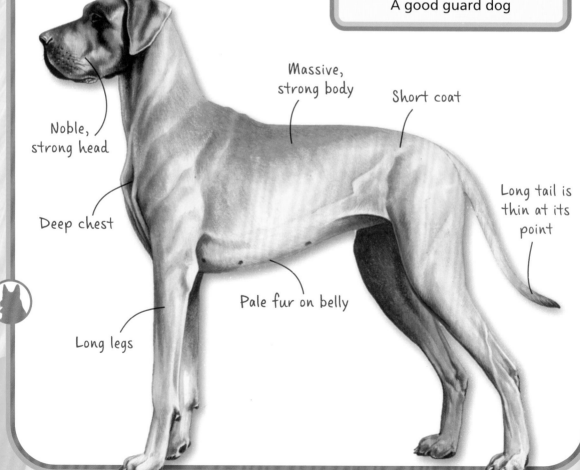

Noble, strong head

Deep chest

Long legs

Pale fur on belly

Massive, strong body

Short coat

Long tail is thin at its point

50

HUNGARIAN PULI

Despite their distinctive appearance, **Pulis were bred as working dogs.** They needed thick, warm coats to live and work in the cold outdoors, where they herded sheep. Today, the Puli coat is a great attraction, but owners have to devote lots of time to combing it, to prevent the fur becoming knotted. Pulis are friendly and well-behaved.

SCALE

These woolly dogs look very similar to another Hungarian breed, the Komondor, which is taller with a height of at least 65 cm.

FACT FILE

Height 37–44 cm

Colour Black, grey, fawn or apricot

Characteristics Obedient and affectionate

Special feature Can be used as a sheep dog

Ears are hidden by fur

Stocky, firm body is hidden beneath the coat

Tail is carried over the back

Thick fur forms cords

Short, round paws

OLD ENGLISH SHEEPDOG

Like most working dogs, Old English Sheepdogs have strong personalities. They can be very loyal and good-tempered, but can also be quick to snap or bark if teased. This large breed was first developed to herd sheep, but is now popular as a pet and a show dog. Its thick, fluffy coat is very attractive, but it requires a lot of grooming to stop it becoming matted.

SCALE

Old English Sheepdogs often have a haircut in summer. Long ago, the cut hair was added to wool and made into clothes.

FACT FILE

Height 56–71 cm

Colour Grey or blue, often with white markings

Characteristics Excitable and cheerful

Special feature Thick, shaggy coat

Eyes are often hidden behind fur

Small ears are hidden beneath fur

Thickset, sturdy body

Strong jaws

Long, fluffy fur

Creamy-white fur on chest

Muscular legs

PEMBROKE WELSH CORGI

These dogs were once known for having short tempers and nipping people. Today, they are friendly dogs that are interested in the world around them and enjoy being with people. Corgis were originally bred to herd cattle, and they still need plenty of time outdoors. They should be trained to learn obedience and patience. Like other short-legged dogs, Corgis do not like climbing stairs, as it can cause them back pain.

SCALE

There are two types of Welsh Corgi – Pembrokes and Cardigans. The two types may look similar, but they have different origins – Cardigans are an older breed.

FACT FILE

Height 25–30 cm

Colour Usually orange or red with white markings

Characteristics Energetic

Special feature Very short legs

Large, erect ears

Alert expression

Thick, fluffy tail

White fur on chest

Short legs with oval paws

Medium-length fur

SAINT BERNARD

Large Saint Bernards were used as herding and rescue dogs. They became especially famous for their work in the snowy Alps, where they were used to find travellers who had become lost. Today, Saint Bernards are mostly kept as pets, even though they are huge. Many Saint Bernards only live to the age of six or seven years. These massive dogs can be hard to handle, although they have sweet natures.

SCALE

Barry was a famous Saint Bernard that died in 1814. According to legend, he saved more than 40 lives, including a boy that he pulled from a heavy snowfall.

FACT FILE

Height Up to 91 cm

Colour Orange, red, tan with white markings

Characteristics Trusting

Special feature Can be used in search and rescue

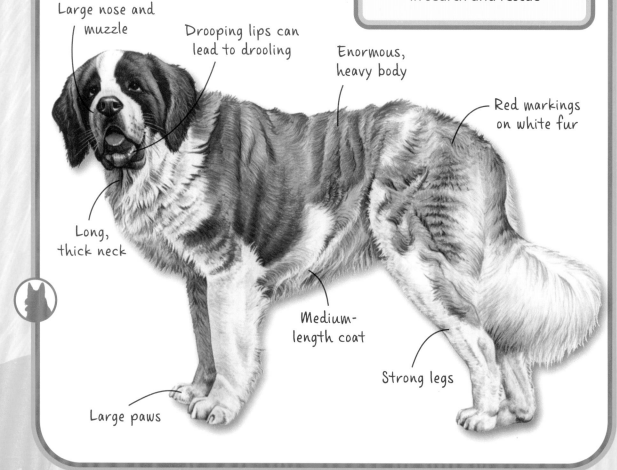

Large nose and muzzle

Drooping lips can lead to drooling

Enormous, heavy body

Red markings on white fur

Long, thick neck

Medium-length coat

Strong legs

Large paws

SIBERIAN HUSKY

When you watch a Husky it is easy to remember that all tame **dogs are descended from wolves.** Although these dogs can become family pets, they are also working dogs that have strong characters. Siberian Huskies are usually kept in a pack and they pull sleds along snow and ice. They will obey their owners, but their loyalty to the pack is just as strong. Huskies howl more often than they bark.

SCALE

Huskies are suited to Siberia, a huge Russian territory that reaches into the Arctic Circle, where the summer lasts less than a month in places.

FACT FILE

Height 51–60 cm

Colour Usually white with dark markings

Characteristics Independent and demanding

Special feature Strong enough to pull sleds

Alert ears

Slender muzzle

Strong, straight, sturdy body

Double-layered, thick coat

Deep chest

Furry tail

Muscular legs

GLOSSARY

Amber This honey-yellow colour is used to describe some dogs' eyes.

Assistance dog These dogs can be trained to work with people who need help with practical tasks, such as crossing the road.

Breed Dogs belonging to a particular breed are similar in appearance and often have similar personalities.

Blue Used to describe steel-grey fur that appears to have a blue colour.

Companion dog These breeds are kept just to be pets, or companions, to their owners. They are usually very friendly, are small enough to carry and make good family pets.

Fawn Light yellowish-brown fur may be described as fawn.

Feathering Long hair that grows around the ankles and feet.

Fox hunting A traditional country pastime that involves chasing foxes on horseback, using a pack of hounds to follow the foxes' scent.

Groom To brush a dog's fur and keep it looking glossy and clean.

Guard dog These dogs tend to bark at strangers. They like to protect their homes and owners.

Hound A breed of dog that has been developed to hunt and has a good sense of smell.

Litter A female dog can give birth to a number of puppies at a time. The collective term is a litter.

Liver Reddish-brown fur may be described as liver.

Matted Fur that has become knotted or tangled.

Muzzle The long nose and mouth of a dog.

Pack animal Some animals like to live in groups called packs. Wild dogs are pack animals and some breeds of dog are pack animals too.

Red Fur that is a vibrant reddish-brown is described as red.

Rescue dog These dogs are trained to help find people using smell and sound. They can find people trapped by avalanches or collapsed buildings.

Show dog A dog kept to compete in dog shows or other competitions.

Sniffer dog These dogs have an exceptionally good sense of smell. They are used to find drugs, food, explosives or other substances.

Spaniel Breeds with long silky coats and drooping ears.

Tan This is a golden-brown colour that is sometimes used to describe dogs' fur.

Terrier These are breeds of small dogs that were developed to get foxes and other small animals out of their burrows.